SUPERSTARS OF BASEBALL

BARTOLO COLÓN

THE RISE TO THE TOP!

Bartolo returns stronger than ever with the Yankees.

2011

Travels to the Dominican Republic for shoulder surgery.

2009

Bartolo is a free agent.

2007

Colón is traded to the Montreal Expos

2002

Plays his first season in the Major Leagues.

1997

The Cleveland Indians sign a contract with Bartolo.

1993

Bartolo Colón is born in Altamira in the Dominican Republic.

1973

Mason Crest
370 Reed Road
Broomall, Pennsylvania 19008
www.masoncrest.com

Printed and bound in the United States of America.

First printing
9 8 7 6 5 4 3 2 1

Library of Congress Cataloging-in-Publication Data

Rodríguez Gonzalez, Tania.
 Bartolo Colón / by Tania Rodriguez.
    p. cm.
Includes index.
ISBN 978-1-4222-2687-2 (hardcover) -- ISBN 978-1-4222-2670-4 (series
hardcover) -- ISBN 978-1-4222-9176-4 (ebook)
 1. Colón, Bartolo, 1973---Juvenile literature. 2. Hispanic American baseball
players--Biography--Juvenile literature. I. Title.
 GV865.C6438R63 2012
 796.357092--dc23
 [B]
                                              2012020931

Produced by Harding House Publishing Services, Inc.
www.hardinghousepages.com

Picture Credits:
Andre Blais | Dreamstime.com: p. 9
Conde | Dreamstime.com: p. 6
Josh Hallett: p. 10
Keith Allison: p. 17, 25, 27
Luis Silvestre: p. 7
Mangin, Brad: p. 1, 2, 15, 16, 18, 20, 22, 24, 28
Peter Lewis | Dreamstime.com: p. 4
All baseball card images courtesy of the Dennis Purdy collection.

BARTOLO COLÓN

Chapter 1

Baseball, the Dominican Republic, and Bartolo Colón

Bartolo Colón has had a great career in baseball. He has pitched in the *All-Star game* and in the *playoffs*. He has won awards and made millions of dollars. Many other players could only dream of doing the things Colón has done in his time in baseball.

Colón's path to playing in the *Major Leagues* began many years ago. Colón has come a long way from the small Dominican town where he was born—but it was his homeland that helped to make him the amazing player he is today. He longed to play in the big leagues as a child, and today, he's living that dream. But like many Dominican baseball players, his road wasn't always easy.

Dominican Baseball — the Good and the Bad

Imagine it's a hot, sunny day on the island. A crowd of spectators is crowded around a baseball diamond that was once a sugarcane field, watching some young boys audition for the chance to one day play baseball in the Big Leagues. Younger boys crowd around the backstop, their noses poking through the chain links; they're all dreaming of the day when it will be their chance to be out their on the field. The **scouts** watch carefully, muttering comments, scribbling notes on their roster sheets.

The coaches—the "buscones"—are watching even more carefully. After all, they have invested thousands of dollars and countless hours in these boys. If any of the players are offered a deal with the Major Leagues, the buscones will get at least 30 percent of the signing bonus. With bonuses being more than a million dollars for the best prospects, that's a sizable chunk of cash!

Every baseball fan knows the fairy tale about the Dominican boy who grew up barefoot, using a milk carton for a baseball glove, a broom handle for a bat, and rolled up socks or lemons for balls—and somehow was transformed into a "Big Papi," a Vlad Guerrero, or a Bartolo Colón. But the fairy godmother in this tale—the one who makes this magical transformation take place—is

Bartolo used to be just a little boy playing baseball in the Dominican Republic.

The Dominican Republic might have a lot of poverty, but it also is rich in culture.

the buscón, and he's sometimes as much a villain as a savior.

Buscones often lie about their players ages. (Legally, a boy can't be **signed** by a Major League team until he's at least 16.) They sometimes keep the boys out of school and inject them with steroids to make them grow bigger. The buscones may take most of the boys' signing bonuses, without the boys even knowing. Sometimes, they bribe the scouts. Several scouts and officials from the Yankees, Red Sox, and Nationals have even lost their jobs because of their dealings with buscones.

Cubans first brought baseball to the island in the 1880s, and it had became the national pastime by the 1940s. But until 1961, only eight Dominicans had played in the Major Leagues, compared to 87 big leaguers who were born in Cuba. Then Cuba became communist, separating itself from the United States—and the Dominican Republic had its chance to shine in the baseball world.

"I'm not sure why I started it," says Epy Guerrero, who founded his country's first baseball academy, in Villa Mella in 1973. "Perhaps it was an inspiration from God. I thought to myself, If these kids had some guidance, maybe they could succeed."

A former **minor leaguer**, Guerrero came up with the idea while scouting for

Steroids

For many professional players, the pressure to perform well is intense. Athletes face stress from everyone around them to constantly improve their skill, strength, and speed in the game of baseball. From the fans who want their favorite players to win and score good stats, to the coaches and team managers who push their players to perform to their maximum potential, to the players themselves, who are surrounded by other world-class athletes and feel the need to overcome them, the pressure to excel is extreme. Often, an athlete turns to chemical enhancements to reach a level of competitive play that he would not normally be capable of. This is never legal, and is almost always dangerous, but nevertheless, many Major League players feel compelled to participate in performance-enhancing drug use.

The most common performance enhancers are anabolic steroids. These chemicals are similar to testosterone, which is the male hormone naturally produced by the body to help stimulate muscle growth. That's why when a player takes anabolic steroids, he receives a boost to his speed and strength that is greater than what the body could normally produce on its own. Major League Baseball (MLB), as well as almost every other organized sport, considers this cheating.

Steroids can cause an unhealthy increase in cholesterol levels and an increase in blood pressure. This stresses the heart, and leads to an increased risk of heart disease. Large doses of steroids can also lead to liver failure, and they have a negative effect on blood sugar levels, sometimes causing problems similar to diabetes.

If an adolescent (typically someone under the age of about 17) takes anabolic steroids, the risks are often much worse. Steroids stop bones from growing, which results in stunted growth. In addition, the risks to the liver and heart are much greater, since a young person's liver and heart are not fully matured and are more susceptible to the damage that steroids can cause. Furthermore, taking steroids puts you at a greater risk of psychological problems that generally begin with aggression but often lead to much more serious issues. Considering these health risks, as well as the fact that anabolic steroids are almost universally banned from organized sports, they should not be used, except by those who have legitimate medical conditions that require their use.

the Astros. The academy started out as just a small field and a house for himself and his players in a patch of cleared jungle—but by 1978, the Toronto Blue Jays were using his expanding facility. Guerrero signed more than 60 players

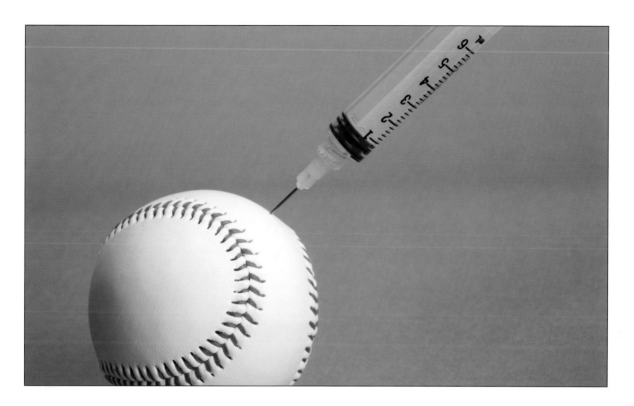

A baseball player that takes anabolic steroids gets a boost in how fast and how strong he is—but it's cheating!

who reached the Major Leagues, and other teams started to pay attention, especially the Dodgers. Today, 29 Major League teams have Dominican academies, but the Dodgers' facility, built on what had once been a sugarcane field, was the first of its kind.

At first, teams would sign players for $2,000, with a $500 tip to the buscón, but that changed in the 1990s when pitcher Ricardo Aramboles was signed for $1 million. Suddenly, top prospects were now worth six or even seven figures—and buscones could make real money, opening the door to greedy individuals ready to take advantage of the system.

Today, however, as people around the world pay more and more attention to Dominican baseball, more buscones are operating like legitimate agents and trainers. Rob Ruck, author of a book on Dominican baseball called *The Tropic of Baseball*, says, "Some of the buscones are really jackals and squeeze whatever they can from the players. But others are maximizing the chances of kids who don't have ideal alternatives."

And despite the corruption, the fairy tales do come true for some lucky boys, boys like Bartolo Colón who make it big in the world of baseball.

Chapter 2

STARTING OUT

Bartolo Colón was born on May 24, 1973, in Altamira in the Dominican Republic. Only a few thousand people live in Altamira, and Bartolo's family lived in a house with no running water. The family didn't have any electricity in their home either.

Bartolo's father, Miguel, worked on a farm, and sometimes Bartolo helped his father work in the fields and fruit groves. His father taught him to work hard—and Bartolo also learned to love baseball from his

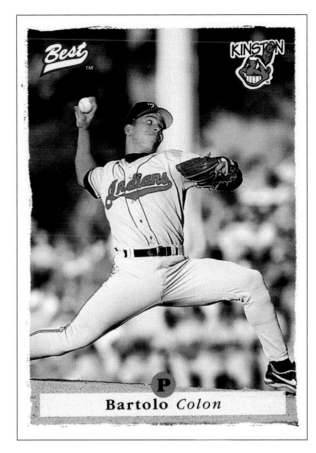

In 1994, Colón played for the Kingston Indians, in the Class A Carolina League.

father. At an early age, Bartolo played as much as he could. Bartolo got better and better as he played more, too.

When he was a teenager, Bartolo worked even harder to get the attention of Major League scouts. In 1989, a scout from Cleveland saw him play in a youth league game. But the scout didn't give Bartolo a **contract**, and Bartolo was worried he would never be signed to play with the Major Leagues.

Then, in 1993, the Cleveland Indians signed Bartolo to a minor league contract. Bartolo had said that he was 18 years old, when really, he was 20 years old. Bartolo wanted to seem like a better player because he was younger. The truth didn't come out until 2002.

Bartolo had his chance now to play baseball for a living, his chance to make it to the Major Leagues. Bartolo was on his way to making his dream come true.

Colón got his first chance to play in 1994 when Cleveland had him start in the **Rookie** League. Colón would have to work his way up

With the Indians, Colón finally made it to the Majors, his childhood dream.

through the Cleveland farm teams. He'd have to work hard. But Colón had his chance to play in the MLB. And he wouldn't waste it.

Playing in the Minors

Colón played for Burlington Indians in the 1994 season. He pitched in 12 games and his earned run average was 3.14.

In 1995, Colón had a great year playing for the Kingston Indians. The Indians play in the Single-A Carolina League, and Colón pitched 21 games for the team. His ERA was 1.96 in 1995, and at the end of the 1995 season, he was named the Carolina League's Pitcher of the Year.

The next year, in 1996, Colón played for two teams. He started the season with the Canton-Akron Indians, a Double-A team. Colón pitched in 13 games for the team, and in 62 innings, he allowed 44

hits. His ERA was 1.74. Later in the season, he moved to the Buffalo Bisons and pitched another eight games.

Moving to the Majors

In the 1997 season, Colón finally got his chance to play in the big leagues. He started the season with the Buffalo Bisons, but he only pitched in 10 games for the Bisons. After that, Cleveland called him up to the Majors. Colón pitched for the Cleveland Indians in 19 games in 1997. His ERA was 5.65 during that time.

Colón had made it into the Majors. He'd dreamed of playing pro baseball since he was a little boy. Now, he was living that dream. Colón was ready to show how good a pitcher he could be, too. He was ready to do his best in the 1998 season.

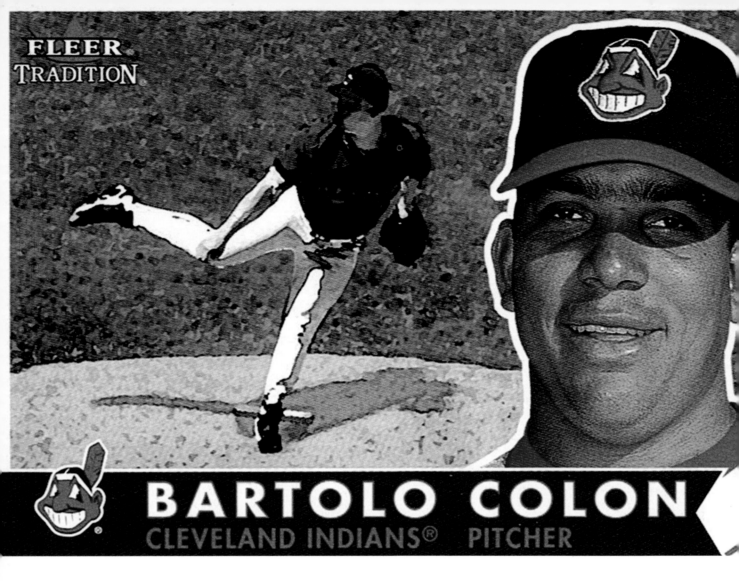

BARTOLO COLON
CLEVELAND INDIANS® PITCHER

Chapter 3

Colón in
Cleveland

Colón worked hard to make it to the Major Leagues.
He had played well for years in the minors, and
now he would play his first full season with the
Cleveland Indians.

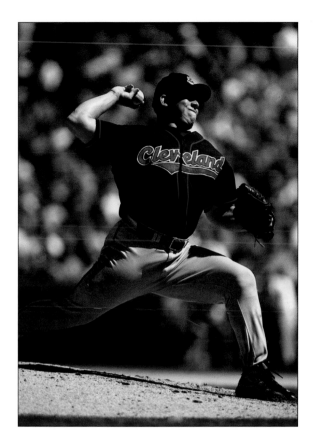

In 1998, Colón pitched 31 games for the Indians, with an ERA of 3.71.

Playing for Cleveland

In the 1998 season, Colón pitched in 31 games for the Indians. He had 158 strikeouts, and his ERA was 3.71. He played so well he was chosen to play in his first All-Star game that year.

The Indians did very well in 1998 as well. The team won 89 games and lost 73 during the regular season, and they finished first in the American League Central *Division*. In the American League Division Series, the Indians beat the Boston Red Sox. Then, in the

American League Championship Series, the Indians faced the New York Yankees. The Yankees beat Cleveland, 4–2—and the Indians' great season was over.

In 1999, Colón pitched in 32 games for Cleveland, with an ERA of 3.95; he had 161 strikeouts during the season. The Indians had another big year in 1999. The team won 97 games and lost 65, and they finished first in the American League Central division for the second year in a row. The team went on to play against the Red Sox again in the American League Division Series, but this time, the Red Sox beat the Indians, 3–2. Colón's second MLB postseason was over.

In the 2000 season, Colón pitched in 30 games with 212 strikeouts and an ERA of 3.88. Meanwhile, the Indians didn't do as well in 2000 as they had in 1999. The team finished second in the AL Central. They didn't make it to the playoff this time. The team would have to try again in 2001.

During the 2001 season, Colón's last full season with Cleveland, he pitched in 34 games for the Indians and 201 strikeouts, with an ERA of 4.09. The Indians did better in the 2001 season, winning 91 games and losing 71. They finished first in the American League Central Division. This time, in the division series, they played the

Colón started 2002 pitching for the Cleveland Indians.

In 2003, Colón had another new team—the Chicago White Sox.

Seattle Mariners. The series lasted for five games, but in the end, the Mariners beat the Indians, 3–2. Cleveland's season was over—and they hadn't made it to the World Series yet again.

Moving Teams

The next year, in 2002, Colón began the season with the Cleveland Indians. He pitched in 16 games for Cleveland, but midway through the season, the team *traded* Colón to the Montreal Expos, and Colón finished the season with the Expos. He pitched in 17 games for Montreal, and his ERA was 2.93 with 149 strikeouts.

Then, early in 2003, Montreal traded Colón again, this time to the Chicago White Sox. Colón pitched in 34 games for the White Sox, with an ERA of 3.87 and 173 strikeouts.

After the 2003 season, Colón became a free agent. He'd been with three teams in two seasons—and now he was headed to yet another team for the 2004 season.

17

Chapter 4

MOVING TO LOS ANGELES

He ended up signing with the Los Angeles Angels. Colón agreed to play for the Angels for four seasons—and the team agreed to pay Colón $51 million for the four years. Colón and his family were excited. The boy from the Dominican countryside was now a millionaire!

Playing in L.A.

In the 2004 season, Colón started slow. But by the middle of the summer, he was doing much better. He pitched in 34 games and finished the regular season with 158 strikeouts. His ERA was 5.01.

The Angels did very well in 2004 as well, winning 92 games and losing 70. The Angels finished first in the American League West division and played the Boston Red Sox in the American League Division Series. Unfortunately, the Red Sox beat the Angels in three games.

In 2005, however, Colón had another great season, and so did the Angels. He pitched in 33 games for the Angels in the regular season, with 157 strikeouts and an ERA of 3.48. Colón was chosen to be in the All-Star game, and at the end of the regular season, he won the American League Cy Young Award, too. Meanwhile, his team won 95 games and lost 67 games during the regular season. They finished first in the American League West Division, and went on to play against the New York Yankees in the division series.

The Angels beat the Yankees, three games to two. In the championship series, though, the Angels lost to the White Sox. Chicago went on to win the World Series.

Colón hurt his shoulder in a 2005 American League Division Series game against the Yankees. Because of his injury,

Colón signed a contract with the Angels for $51 million.

he couldn't play much in 2006. He pitched in only 10 games during the entire season.

The Angels did well without him but not as well as they had in 2005. The team won 89 games and lost 69, but they came in second place in the American League West.

Colón's shoulder was still bothering him the next year. He pitched in 19 games for the Angels and 76 strikeouts during the 2007 season. His ERA was 6.34.

2007 was a hard year, but Colón still proved his talent.

The Angels did better in 2007 than they had in 2006. The team finished first in the America League West with 94 wins and 68 losses, and the Angel played against the Red Sox in the division series. The Red Sox beat the Angels in just three games, though.

Moving Around

After the 2007 season, Colón became a *free agent*. His shoulder was giving him a lot of pain, and he just couldn't play the way he had. In February 2008, he signed a minor league contract with the Boston Red Sox. Colón started the season with a Red Sox farm team. After he threw a one-hitter in a May game, the Red Sox called Colón back up to the Majors. He had proved that he was still an amazing pitcher, even with an aching shoulder! He finished the rest of the season with Boston.

In September, Colón left the Red Sox and went to the Dominican Republic. He was tired and he wanted to go home. At first, he had intended to just go for a short

Colón plays for his country against Cuba in the "World Baseball Classic."

visit, but then he stayed longer. He told the team he had to take care of some personal business.

The Red Sox were angry with Colón. They suspended him and then put him on the restricted list. His time with the Red Sox was over. Colón was a free agent again.

Early in 2009, Colón signed to the Chicago White Sox again. He agreed to play for the team for one year, and Chicago agreed to pay Colón $1 million for the 2009 season. Colón pitched 12 games for the White Sox in 2009, with an ERA of 4.19 and 38 strikeouts. Then his season ended early when he hurt his arm and shoulder yet again.

Colón's injury was bad. He'd need to have surgery if he ever hoped to play again.

Chapter 5

BARTOLO COLÓN TODAY

Colón ended up having groundbreaking surgery on his damaged right arm. The surgeon took fat from his own body, extracted "stem cells" from that fat, and then injected the cells into his shoulder. The cells from his own body helped his shoulder repair itself and heal.

When people found out that Colón had had this surgery, they wondered if it was legal. They suspected that he might have used hormones or steroids as part of his treatment, which are banned in the United States. (Colón had his surgery done in the Dominican Republic.) But the doctors who performed the surgery were respected experts in their field, and they insisted that they had used no illegal substances in Colón's treatment.

Despite the controversy, other players were excited about the possibilities of this type of surgery. Other pitchers with injured shoulders started lining up to have the same procedure. They knew it could make all the difference in their careers if they could use their own bodies' cells to heal their injured shoulders.

Playing for the Yankees

Meanwhile, Colón was back, ready to play. In January 2011, he signed with the New York Yankees, but the contract was a minor league deal. He would have to prove at winter training if he was really ready to play on the Yankees in the 2011 season.

Colón wanted to prove to the Yankees that he was truly ready to handle the Major Leagues again, so he gave Tony Peña, the Yankees bench coach, a call. He pleaded with Peña to give him a chance to

pitch. Peña agreed to test him with about 60 pitches in a simulated game.

"He threw five innings first," Peña said. "Then he got better and better. I saw him throwing pitches better than he did before. Before, he was a power pitcher, just throwing, but now he was locating pitches, throwing a two-seam fastball, really being a pitcher. That's when I made the call to the [Yankees]. The rest is history."

Colón made it onto the Yankees' roster for opening day, and he spent the rest

Yankee's bench coach Tony Peña.

25

Bartolo Colón has proven to the world that his baseball career isn't over yet!

of the season with the Yankees. He pitched in 29 games and had 135 strike-outs during the regular season, with an ERA of 4.00. He even pitched one shutout! His shoulder was definitely back to normal—and so was Bartolo Colón!

The Yankees had a great season in 2011 as well, finishing first in the American League East division after win-

ning 97 games and losing 65. In the division series, the Yankees played the Detroit Tigers. The Tigers won the series after five games, and Colón's first season with the Yankees was over.

But Colón had proved to the world that his baseball career wasn't over. At the end of the 2009 season, the White Sox were glad to be rid of him. They thought

Bartolo Colón still has games to play and awards to win. Who knows what's next!

he was a has-been player whose talent was all used up. But now the Yankees were excited to have him.

"I think he's been our glue," Yankee pitching coach Larry Rothschild said of Colón.

Yankee *manager* Joe Girardi agreed. "He's been huge for us. We had no expectations in spring training—and he turned out to be the biggest surprise of spring for us."

What's Next?

Bartolo Colón has done great things in baseball, and now he's made an amazing comeback. But baseball isn't the only thing important to him. His family and his hometown back in the Dominican Republic are very important to him, as well.

Colón lives with his wife Rosanna in New York State. The couple has three sons. But even though he lives in the United States, Colón has never forgotten his hometown. He does a lot of charity work for Altamira.

Colón worked hard to go from dreaming about playing baseball to playing in the MLB. He spent years getting better and better in the minors. Then he had to find a way to overcome serious injuries that threatened to put an end to his career. Today, Colón has made it to the top of the baseball world. Still, he has goals he hasn't reached. He still hasn't pitched in a World Series. He still has games to win and awards to get.

No one can know what will happen next for Bartolo Colón. One thing is for sure, though. He'll work hard to succeed in baseball. Colón will try his best whenever he's on the mound. And his fans will always be there to watch!

Find Out More

Online

Baseball Almanac

www.baseball-almanac.com

Baseball Hall of Fame

baseballhall.org

Baseball Reference

www.baseball-reference.com

Dominican Baseball

mlb.mlb.com/mlb/features/dr/
index.jsp

History of Baseball

www.19cbaseball.com

Major League Baseball

www.mlb.com

Science of Baseball

www.exploratorium.edu/baseball

In Books

Augustin, Bryan. *The Dominican Republic From A to Z.* New York: Scholastic, 2005.

Jacobs, Greg. *The Everything Kids' Baseball Book.* Avon, Mass.: F+W Media, 2012.

Kurlansky, Mark. *The Eastern Stars: How Baseball Changed the Dominican Town of San Pedro de Macorís.* New York: Riverhead Books, 2010.

Glossary

All-Star Game: The game played in July between the best players from each of the two leagues within the MLB.

batting average: A statistic that measures how good a batter is, which is calculated by dividing the number of hits a player gets by how many times he is at bat.

contract: A written promise between a player and the team. It tells how much he will be paid for how long.

culture: The way of life of a group of people, which includes things like values and beliefs, language, food, and art.

defense: Playing to keep the other team from scoring; includes the outfield and infield positions, pitcher, and catcher.

disabled list: A list of players who are injured and can't play for a certain period of time.

division: A group of teams that plays one another to compete for the championship; in the MLB, divisions are based on geographic regions.

free agent: A player who does not currently have a contract with any team.

general manager: The person in charge of a baseball team, who is responsible for guiding the team to do well.

heritage: Something passed down by previous generations.

Major League Baseball (MLB): The highest level of professional baseball in the United States and Canada.

minor leagues: The level of professional baseball right below the Major Leagues.

Most Valuable Player (MVP): The athlete who is named the best player for a certain period of time.

offense: Playing to score runs at bat.

playoffs: A series of games played after the regular season ends, to determine who will win the championship.

professional: The level of baseball in which players get paid.

rookie: A player in his first-year in the MLB.

runs batted in (RBI): The number of points that a player gets for his team by hitting the ball.

scouts: People who find the best young baseball players to sign to teams.

sign: To agree to a contract between a baseball player and a team.

trade: An agreement with another team that gives a player in return for a player from the other team.

Index